Reader's Clubhouse

A TRUCK CAN HELP

BR
Schmauss
2006

By Judy Kentor Schmauss

Table of Contents

© Copyright 2006 by Barron's Educational Series, Inc.

All inquiries should be addressed to:
Barron's Educational Series, Inc.
250 Wireless Boulevard
Hauppauge, New York 11788
www.barronseduc.com

Library of Congress Control Number: 2005043502

ISBN-13: 978-0-7641-3290-2
ISBN-10: 0-7641-3290-3

Library of Congress Cataloging-in-Publication Data
Schmauss, Judy Kentor.
    A truck can help / Judy Kentor Schmauss.
        p. cm. – (Reader's clubhouse)
    Includes bibliographical references and index.
    ISBN-13: 978-0-7641-3290-2
    ISBN-10: 0-7641-3290-3
    1. Trucks—Juvenile literature. I. Title. II. Series.

TL230.15.S36 2006
629.224—dc22

                                                                    2005043502

Date of Manufacture: March 2012
Manufactured by: L08E08O, Guangdong, China

9 8 7 6 5 4 3 2

Dear Parent and Educator,

Welcome to the Barron's Reader's Clubhouse, a series of books that provide a phonics approach to reading.

Phonics is the relationship between letters and sounds. It is a system that teaches children that letters have specific sounds. Level 1 books introduce the short-vowel sounds. Level 2 books progress to the long-vowel sounds. This progression matches how phonics is taught in many classrooms.

A Truck Can Help reviews the short-vowel sounds introduced in previous Level 1 books. Simple words with these short-vowel sounds are called **decodable words.** The child knows how to sound out these words because he or she has learned the sounds they include. This story also contains **high-frequency words.** These are common, everyday words that the child learns to read by sight. High-frequency words help ensure fluency and comprehension. **Challenging words** go a little beyond the reading level. The child will identify these words with help from the photograph on the page. All words are listed by their category on page 23.

Here are some coaching and prompting statements you can use to help a young reader read *A Truck Can Help*:

- **On page 5, "jobs" is a decodable word. Point to the word and say:**
  Read this word. How did you know the word? What sounds did it make?

  Note: There are many opportunities to repeat the above instruction throughout the book.

- **On page 12, "fire" is a challenging word. Point to the word and say:**
  Read this word. It rhymes with "tire." How did you know the word? Did you look at the picture? How did it help?

You'll find more coaching ideas on the Reader's Clubhouse Web site: *www.barronsclubhouse.com.* Reader's Clubhouse is designed to teach and reinforce reading skills in a fun way. We hope you enjoy helping children discover their love of reading!

Sincerely,

Nancy Harris

Nancy Harris
Reading Consultant

Big trucks help with big jobs.

A pig must go to a new pen.
Can a truck help?

Yes, this truck can get
pigs to a pen.

Look at this big mess.
Can a truck help?

Yes, a truck can fix this mess.

This pit is big.
Can a truck help?

Yes, dump trucks fill pits.

Look at the fire.
Can a truck help?

Yes, this truck gets there fast.

A van will not go.
Can a truck help?

Yes, this truck has a ramp.

There is no gas at the pump.
Can a truck help?

Yes, this truck gets gas to the pump.

Big trucks help with big jobs.

Fun Facts About
Trucks

- The United States has 36 million trucks. That's more than any other country.

- The biggest truck in the world can pull 400 tons. That's about as much as the weight of 70 elephants!

- In the United States, truck drivers are allowed to drive for only 10 hours at a time so they don't get too tired.

- The first truck was built in Germany, in 1896.

- In England, a truck is called a *lorry.*

Find Out More

Read a Book

Oxlade, Chris. *Trucks (Transportation Around the World)*. Heinemann Library, 2001.

Rogers, Hal. *Tractors*. The Child's World, 2001.

Williams, Linda D. *Dump Trucks*. Capstone Press, 2005.

Visit a Web Site

Kikki's Workshop
http://www.kenkenkikki.jp/e_index.html
Kikki is a curious character who has lots
of information to share about bulldozers,
scoopers, lifters, and many other machines.

Glossary

 **pen** the fenced-in place where a pig lives

 **pit** a big hole in the ground

 **ramp** a slope that connects a high place to a low place

Word List

Challenging Words	fire truck trucks	
Decodable Short-Vowel Words	dump fast fill fix gas has jobs mess	pen pig pigs pit pits ramp van will yes
High-Frequency Words	a at big can get gets go help is look must	new no not pump the there this to with

Index

Photo credits:

Page 4–5: © Reinhard Eisele/Corbis
Page 7: © Chris Sattlberger/Getty Images
Page 9: © Jonathan Nourok/PhotoEdit
Page 12: © Alan Schein Photography/Corbis
Page 13: © Keith Levit Photography/Index Stock Imagery
Page 15: © Tony Freeman/PhotoEdit
Page 16: © Getty Images
Page 22, top: © Jim Sugar/Corbis